Coconut Flour Recipes
Gluten Free, Low-carb and Low GI Alternative to Wheat: High in Fiber and Protein

Contents

About the Book 4

Introduction 5

Chapter 1 6

    Rise and Shine: Breakfast Recipes 6

    Cinnamon Rolls 7

    Bacon, Egg and Cheese Muffins 8

    Apple Banana Berry Baked French Toast mm! 9

    Chocolate Donuts 10

    Cinnamon Sugar Coconut Puffs 11

    Tasty Porridge 12

    Pumpkin Coconut "Oatmeal" 13

    Coffee Cake 14

    Flax & Raisin Breakfast Bread 15

    Sweet Potato Biscuits 16

    Gravy for Biscuits 17

Chapter 2 18

Everyday Breads, Specialty Loaves and Muffins 18

    Bread Loaf 18

    Multiuse Flatbreads 19

    Tortillas 20

    Home-style Corn Bread 21

    Apple Crumbly Bread 22

    Cranberry Walnut Bread Loaf 23

    Pumpkin Bread 24

    Banana Nut Bread Loaf 25

    Jalapeno Bacon Bread Loaf 26

    Blueberry Muffins 27

    Cocoa Banana Muffins 28

    Citrus Orange Cranberry Muffins 29

    Walnut Raisin Muffins 30

Chapter 3 31

Savory Dish Recipes 31

    Meatloaf 31

    Fried Fish 32

    Fried Chicken 33

- Beef Stroganoff 34
- Coconut Crusted Halibut 35
- Herb and Tomato Pizza 36
- Spinach Soufflé 37
- Creamy Chicken Soup 38
- Homemade Hamburger 39
- Coconut Battered Shrimp 40

Chapter 4 41

A Healthier Way to Celebrate: Cakes and Cupcakes 41

- White Cake 41
- Chocolate Cake 42
- Carrot Cake 43
- Strawberry Lime Cake 44
- Lemony Coconut Cake 45
- Vanilla Cupcakes 46
- Fudge Cupcakes 47

Chapter 5 48

Treat Yourself to Healthier Desserts 48

- Pie Crust 48
- Peanut Butter Cups 49
- Strawberry Shortcake Bites 50
- Chocolate Chip Cookies 51
- Walnut Apple Banana Cookies 52
- Sugar Cookies 53
- Brownies 54
- Lemon Coconut Macaroons 55
- Pecan Treats 56
- Cream Tart in a Chocolate Crust 57

About the Book

This book contains recipes that use coconut flour. We will start with recipes for the most important meal of the day, breakfast. Chapter 1 introduces breakfast choices that will not only get your body started off on the right foot, but also taste delicious. The section purposely begins with pancakes, so you can experiment and test the liquid to flour ratio. With pancakes you can mix, test how it cooks and adjust accordingly. In Chapter 2 we will graduate to multi use breads, muffins and specialty loaves. You can incorporate coconut flour breads into sandwiches, wraps and tortillas using these foundational recipes. In Chapter 3 we will introduce you to ways to include coconut flour into savory entree dishes. See what surprising dishes have healthier alternatives. After dinner we will move on to cakes in Chapter 4. When it comes time for family and friends to celebrate, refined flour and sugar desserts will get the boot after giving these recipes a try. Create a healthier cake, without sacrificing taste. Last but not least, in Chapter 5 you will find flavorful delicious desserts with nutritious makings.

Introduction

Enjoy a healthier version of indulgent recipes by substituting coconut flour for regular flour. These recipes are great for those who have dietary restrictions, as well as those who want a nutritious alternate of their favorite recipes. Coconut flour is dried and ground into a fine powder from the coconut meat left over after the production of coconut milk. It is light, very absorbent, wheat free and gluten free. While you are enjoying your favorite foods you will benefit from high fiber content (60%), low carbohydrates, and rich protein content (40%). Coconut boasts benefits from lauric acid and manganese which help the thyroid, skin health, better utilization of nutrients from other foods and stabilization of blood sugar levels.

There are a few coconut flour facts that are good to know before jumping into any recipes. The flour is very dry and absorbs a lot of moisture keeping your baked goods moist longer. Most recipes use a lot of eggs as a result of the absorbency, which gives the batter structure. A small amount of coconut flour also goes a long way and creates a thick consistency. It is naturally sweet which reduces the amount of sweetener needed in many recipes. It does have a strong smell and taste but is covered well by chocolate, garlic and onions. Many recipes play up the flavor of coconut and add coconut milk, oil and/or shredded pieces. Other ingredients needed in many recipes include coconut oil, honey, vanilla, stevia, raw honey, eggs, eggs and more eggs! So we recommend to stock up on these items as well as your coconut flour when shopping. Enjoy this exciting new ingredient that makes the most delicious indulgences a healthier possibility!

Chapter 1
Rise and Shine: Breakfast Recipes

Pancakes

1/4 cup coconut flour
2 egg whites
1/2 cup almond milk
1 teaspoon vanilla
1/2 teaspoon baking powder
1/8 teaspoon salt
1/8 teaspoon cinnamon
Stevia (I use 1-2 packets.)
Mashed banana/blueberries (optional)

Heat up a greased nonstick skillet over medium high heat for a few minutes while you combine all ingredients and stir until completely combined. Pour about 2 tablespoons of your batter into the skillet for a medium pancake. Cook until golden brown on both sides and remove pancake from pan. Grease your pan between each pancake.

Cinnamon Rolls

The Dough:
1/2 cup coconut flour
2 egg whites
1 teaspoon xanthan gum
1/2 teaspoon baking powder
5 tablespoons water
Dash of salt
Sprinkle of stevia (Optional)

Filling:
2 packets stevia (Or one teaspoon honey or agave)
2 tablespoons ground cinnamon
2 tablespoons ground almonds (ground hazelnut works, too)
2 tablespoons water

Preheat oven to 380F. Mix all the dough ingredients together in a bowl very well. Roll the dough into a ball and flatten it out until thin using a rolling pin sprinkled in coconut flour. Next combine all the filling ingredients together in a bowl and spread it out on top of the dough evenly. Cut with a knife into three sections. Roll each section up and trim ends. Bake for 20-25 minutes until lightly browned. Allow them to cool and then slice into rolls and enjoy.

Bacon, Egg and Cheese Muffins

3 tablespoons coconut flour
6 strips bacon
3 eggs
1/4 teaspoon salt
1/4 teaspoons baking powder
4 ounces cheddar cheese, shredded/diced
Coconut oil to grease muffin tin

Preheat your oven to 400F and grease your muffin tin with the coconut oil. Fry your bacon in a skillet until crispy and put aside. In a mixing bowl combine eggs, bacon drippings and salt and mix well. Next add in coconut flour and baking powder and mix until there are no lumps. After your batter is smooth, crumble up the bacon and fold it into the batter along with the cheese. Mix thoroughly, pour into muffin tin and bake for 15 minutes. Enjoy this filling, balanced start to your day.

Apple Banana Berry Baked French Toast mm!

1/2 cup coconut flour
8 eggs
2 teaspoons coconut oil
6 apples
1/3 full fat coconut milk
4 mashed bananas
1 cup raspberries
1 teaspoon baking soda
1 teaspoon salt
1 teaspoon cinnamon

Preheat your oven to 350F and grease your 9x13 baking dish. Start by slicing the apples into 1/8ths. Heat up coconut oil and sauté the apples with cinnamon to taste until lightly browned and then set aside. In a bowl combine the dry ingredients (coconut flour, salt, baking soda and cinnamon). Then combine the wet ingredients in a separate bowl (eggs, mashed bananas, coconut milk and vanilla.) Now add the dry ingredients into the wet and stir until blended well. Lastly, you will finish your batter by folding in the berry goodness. Now arrange the sautéed apples in the bottom of the dish and pour the batter on top of them. Bake for 45-55 minutes until the top is golden brown. Top off this delicious breakfast with berries. Butter and maple syrup!

Chocolate Donuts

Standard donut pan
1/4 cup coconut flour
3 eggs
1/4 cup cocoa powder
1/8 teaspoon sea salt
1/2 teaspoon baking soda
1/4 cup coconut oil, melted
1/3 cup pure maple syrup
1 tablespoon vanilla extract

Chocolate Glaze
1/2 cup dark chocolate chips
2 tablespoons coconut oil

Preheat your oven to 350F and generously cover your pan with coconut oil. Mix together your dry ingredients in a medium bowl (coconut flour, cocoa powder, sea salt and baking soda). Next whisk in your wet ingredients (eggs, coconut oil, maple syrup, and vanilla). Mix until the batter is smooth and thoroughly mixed. You will need to transfer the batter to a plastic bag, cut the corner off, and squeeze into the donut pan spaces. Bake these until firm for 18-20 minutes and then allow to cool completely on a wire rack for 15 minutes. Melt the chocolate chips and oil in a pan and dip the donuts into the glaze. It will solidify as it cools and make for a very tasty, healthier alternative to your donut cravings.

Cinnamon Sugar Coconut Puffs

3 tablespoons coconut flour
1 1/4 cups almond flour
2 tablespoons coconut palm sugar
1/4 sea salt
1 egg white
1 tablespoon cinnamon
1/3 cup honey
3 tablespoons of coconut oil

Preheat your oven 350 degrees and line baking sheet with parchment paper. Combine all dry ingredients (almond flour, coconut flour, palm sugar, cinnamon and salt.) in another bowl combine all wet ingredients (egg white, honey, coconut oil.)When mixed well pour wet ingredients into dry ingredients and mix until all lumps are worked out. Next you will use your hands to make small balls out of the batter. The smaller they are, the crunchier they will be. Place in lines on parchment paper and bake for 17 minutes. Let them cool and store in an air tight container. They are very good with fruit!

Tasty Porridge

1 tablespoon coconut flour
1/2 cup water
1/8 tablespoon pure vanilla extract
1/2 cup whole milk
1/4 cup coconut flakes
2 tablespoons wholegrain chia seeds
1 unripe banana
Dash salt
1/3 organic rolled outs
2 tablespoons virgin coconut oil
1 to 2 tablespoons of organic raw honey
2 teaspoons butter

Combine the banana, water and milk. Sprinkle the coconut flour in the mix and mash using a fork. Combine coconut flakes, chia seeds, salt, organic rolled oats, and virgin coconut oil. Bring the mixture to a boil on the stove and then reduce heat while gently mixing. Cool and add butter and honey.

Pumpkin Coconut "Oatmeal"

1 tablespoon coconut flour
1/4 cup coconut
1/2 cup coconut milk, almond milk, or other milk of choice
1/2 cup water
1/4 cup pumpkin puree
1/4 teaspoon cinnamon
1/2 teaspoon vanilla extract
Dash nutmeg
Dash ginger
Stevia, to taste (I used 1 packet.)

Carefully toast the coconut, until golden brown, in a pot over medium heat. After the coconut has been toasted, stir in the milk and water and bring to a boil. Whisk in the pumpkin and bring to a boil, then whisk in the coconut flour and bring to a boil. Cook until desired consistency. Remove from heat and add in vanilla and other spices to taste.

Coffee Cake

For the crumb topping:
1 Tablespoon unsweetened shredded coconut
1/2 Tablespoon almond meal
1 teaspoon applesauce
Pinch salt
Sweetener to taste (I used 1/2 packet of stevia.)
For the cake:
2 Tablespoons coconut flour
1/2 teaspoon baking powder
1/4 teaspoon cinnamon
2 egg whites
1/4 cup applesauce
Sweetener to taste (I use 1-2 packets of stevia.)

Combine all cake ingredients together in a bowl. Mix well. Pour into a greased microwave safe mug. Combine all ingredients for coffee cake crumb topping and sprinkle on top of cake. Microwave for 2 minutes and let cool.

Flax & Raisin Breakfast Bread

3/4 cup coconut flour, plus 1 tablespoon
5 large eggs
1/2 cup ground flax seeds
1/2 cup raisins
1/2 cup melted butter
2 tablespoons plain, full fat yogurt
1/2 teaspoon sea salt
1/4 cup honey

Preheat your oven to 400 degrees and grease a 9x5 inch loaf tin. Whisk together the eggs, honey, yogurt and room temperature butter then stir in the flax seeds. Next add in the raisins with a tablespoon of coconut flour and set aside. In another large bowl mix the coconut flour and salt well and then add the wet ingredients and stir until the batter is runny. Now add in the raisin mixture and pour it into the loaf tin and bake for 30 minutes. Makes for a great, easy breakfast on the go.

Sweet Potato Biscuits

3 tablespoon coconut flour
3 eggs, whisked
1 large sweet potato or yam
3 tablespoons melted butter
1 teaspoon baking powder
1/2 teaspoon garlic powder
Salt and pepper to taste

Preheat oven to 415F. Poke holes in the sweet potato with a fork and bake for 30-40 min. After potato is done baking, reduce oven to 375F. Peel sweet potato and mash in a bowl with a fork. Add eggs and mix well with sweet potato and add melted butter. Then add coconut flour, baking powder, garlic powder, salt and pepper. Next add a cooked, diced jalapeno. Add parchment paper to a baking sheet and drop your biscuits using an ice cream scoop to make them all equal size. Place in oven and bake for 22-27 minutes. Let rest. Top with some melted grass fed butter. Tastes great with gravy!

Gravy for Biscuits

3 teaspoons coconut flour
1 -14 ounce can of coconut milk
1 pound pork breakfast sausage
1/2 teaspoon dried parsley
1/2 teaspoon garlic powder
1/4 teaspoon dried sage
1/8 teaspoon smoke paprika
Salt and pepper

Cook breakfast sausage over medium-high heat until all the pink is gone. Break up the sausage as it cooks. Once the meat is cooked remove using slotted spoon and place in a bowl. Add coconut flour to pork fat teaspoon by teaspoon constantly whisking. Once your mixture is thick, add your coconut milk to the pan and whisk in parsley, garlic powder, sage, smoked paprika, salt and pepper. Mix well. When the flavors meld add the sausage back in. Add salt and pepper to your taste. Pour on top of biscuits.

Chapter 2

Everyday Breads, Specialty Loaves and Muffins

Bread Loaf

3/4 cup coconut flour
6 eggs
1/2 cup melted butter
1-2 tablespoons honey
1/2 teaspoon sea salt

Preheat oven to 350F. Mix all ingredients together and pour into small buttered bread loaf pan. Bake for 40 minutes. Remove loaf from pan and let cool completely, then serve. Also, cut into slices for sandwiches.

Multiuse Flatbreads

1/4 cup coconut flour
1/3 cup tapioca starch
1 cup egg whites (12 eggs)
2 tablespoon palm shortening (or cooking fat)
2 tablespoon apple cider vinegar
1 teaspoon baking powder
1 tablespoon honey
1/2 cup water
1/2 teaspoon salt
1/2 teaspoon onion powder
1/2 teaspoon garlic powder
1 tablespoon caraway seed or ground flaxseed meal

Combine all dry ingredients in a blender and blend on high speed for 20-30 seconds. Move the dry mix to a large bowl and add all other ingredients except for the shortening/oil. Mix well until a thin batter forms. Now preheat a frying pan over low heat while melting your shortening/oil in the microwave. Cover your pan completely, not skipping around the edges. Now to pour the batter. Use a spoon to pour 1/4 cup of the batter into the greased frying pan and spread it to the size you want. Cook it until it is lightly browned and firm on one side. Gently flip over and cook the other side until lightly browned and firm. Between each flatbread cover the pan in shortening/oil again.

Tortillas

1/4 cup coconut flour
8 large egg whites
1/4 teaspoon baking powder
1/2 cup water
Coconut oil for coating pan

Preheat your small non-stick skillet over medium heat and coat the entire pan in 1 teaspoon of coconut oil. Combine all the ingredients together in a bowl and mix until no lumps remain. Once your batter is whisked, pour 2 tablespoon of batter into pan and tilt the pan to spread the batter out to make a think tortilla. The tortilla needs to brown and then you will be able to flip it without ripping it. Brown the opposite side. Repeat until all of the batter is used.

Home-style Corn Bread

1/2 cup of coconut flour
4 eggs
1 cup of water
2 tablespoon apple cider vinegar
1/2 teaspoon of garlic powder
1/4 cup and 1 teaspoon of coconut oil melted
1/4 teaspoon of sea salt
1 teaspoon caraway seeds, ground
1/2 teaspoon baking soda

Preheat the oven to 350F and grease your baking tin. Take the eggs out of the refrigerator so they can come to room temperature. Combine the room temp eggs, apple cider vinegar, water and 1/4 cup of melted coconut oil(not hot, you don't want to cook the eggs) in the blender and blend on low for 30 seconds. Next you will add your coconut flour, garlic powder, salt, ground caraway seeds and baking soda and blend for one minute. Pour the batter into the pan and bake for 40-45 minutes. Get the golden look by rubbing coconut oil on your bread and turning your oven to broil low. Keep an eye on it and pull it out when it reaches the color you want.

Apple Crumbly Bread

1/3 cup coconut flour
2 cups nut/ seed flour
4 eggs separated
1-2 teaspoon cinnamon
1/2 teaspoon salt
1/2 cup butter
1/4 cup honey
1 small banana
1 teaspoon vanilla
3 small apples chopped and peeled

Preheat your oven to 350F and line a 9x5 loaf pan with parchment paper. Combine the flour, cinnamon, and salt in a bowl. Next you will need your food processor to blend the egg white until stiff. Add the egg yolks, butter, honey, banana and vanilla and blend until smooth. Fold 2/3's of the chopped apples into the dry mixture and then pour the wet mixture in and combine well. Pour the bread batter into the pan and bake for 90 minutes or until it springs back. You can cover with aluminum foil to slow down the browning.

Cranberry Walnut Bread Loaf

2/3 cup sifted coconut flour
8 eggs
1/2 cup coconut oil or melted butter
1/2 cup coconut cream
1/2 cup crystallized coconut nectar
1 teaspoon vanilla
1 teaspoon lemon extract
1/s teaspoon salt
1 teaspoon baking powder
1 cup dried cranberries
1/2 cup walnuts chopped

Preheat oven to 350 degrees and grease 9x5x3 inch pan. Blend together eggs, coconut milk, nectar, vanilla, lemon extract and salt. Combine the baking powder and coconut flour together and add to the batter, whisking until there are no lumps. Add in cranberries and nuts. Pour into pan and bake for 60 min. Remove from pan and let cool completely.

Pumpkin Bread

1/2 cup coconut flour
5 eggs
1 teaspoon baking soda
1 cup pumpkin puree
1 tablespoon apple cider vinegar
1 1/2 tablespoons pumpkin spice
1/4 teaspoon sea salt
1/4 cup coconut oil
2 table spoons raw honey
Crushed pecan or walnuts are very tasty (optional)

When the leaves start to fall and scarves come out, the smell and taste of pumpkin bread brings a comfort to the home that is just right. To begin, preheat your oven to 400F. You will need two bowls. Combine all dry ingredients (flour, pumpkin spice, baking soda, salt) in one and all wet ingredients (pumpkin puree, eggs, apple cider vinegar, honey) in the other. Mix each well. Use an electric mixer to whisk the dry ingredients into the wet ingredients. Grease baking dish with coconut oil. Pour batter into dish and smooth the top. Bake for 25 minutes. We recommend an 8x8 inch dish

Banana Nut Bread Loaf

¾ cup sifted coconut flour
1 teaspoon baking powder
8 eggs
1 ripe banana
½ cup coconut milk
½ cup Organic Raw Crystallized Coconut Nectar
½ teaspoon vanilla extract
½ teaspoon almond extract
½ teaspoon salt
½ cup pecans or walnuts, chopped

Preheat oven to 350F and grease 9x5x3 inch loaf pan. Blend together mashed banana, eggs, coconut milk, nectar, salt, vanilla and almond extracts. Combine coconut flour with baking powder and whisk thoroughly into batter until there are no lumps. Fold in nuts. Pour into pan and bake for 60 minutes. Remove from pan and cool on rack.

Jalapeno Bacon Bread Loaf

1/2 cup coconut flour
1/2 teaspoon sea salt
1/4 teaspoon baking soda
1/4 cup of water
4 thick slices of bacon
6 large eggs
1/2 cup butter
3 large jalapenos

Spice up your menu! Preheat your oven to 400F and begin slicing your jalapeno into 2cm slices. Lay those alongside your bacon strips on a cookie sheet. Bake for 10 minutes then remove and lower oven to 375F. After they are roasted allow them to cool, then deseed your jalapenos. Combine the bacon and jalapenos in a food processor and pulse thoroughly. In a separate bowl mix the eggs, water and butter. Then whisk in coconut flour, baking soda and sea salt. After that is mixed well, fold in your bacon and jalapeno mix. Spread batter into greased pan and bake for 40-45 minutes. Insert a toothpick if it comes out clean, the bread is ready.

Blueberry Muffins

Dry ingredients:
1/4 cup coconut flour (sifted)
1/4 teaspoon baking powder
Wet ingredients:
3 eggs
3 tablespoon butter, melted
3 tablespoons honey
1/4 teaspoon salt
1/4 teaspoon vanilla
1/8 teaspoon almond extract
1/2 cup blueberries (make sure they are thoroughly dry)

Preheat oven to 400F. Sift the dry ingredients together. In a separate bowl combine eggs, almond extract, butter, honey, salt and vanilla. Fold the wet ingredients into the dry ingredients until there are no lumps. Add blueberries. Scoop the batter into either cupcake liners or a greased muffin pan filling each spot half way. Bake at 400 for 16-18 minutes.

Cocoa Banana Muffins

1 cup coconut flour
1 1/2 teaspoon baking soda
2/3 cup cocoa powder
1/2 tablespoon butter
1/2 cup brown sugar
6 large eggs
3/4 cup granulated sugar
1/2 cup and 2 tablespoons of sour cream
3 mashed bananas
1 1/2 teaspoon salt
1 1/2 teaspoon baking soda

Preheat oven to 350F. Combine dry ingredients including cocoa, coconut flour, baking soda and salt in a bowl. Combine the butter, eggs and sugar in a separate bowl and mix well then add the sour cream and bananas. Mix the dry ingredients into the wet ingredients and mix until all lumps disappear. Fill either the cupcake liners or greased muffin tins 3/4 full and bake 24-30 minutes.

Citrus Orange Cranberry Muffins

1/4 cup sifted coconut flour
2 tablespoons coconut cream/milk
3 eggs
2 tablespoons orange juice concentrate
3 tablespoons honey
1/4 teaspoon salt
1/8 teaspoon almond extract
1/4 teaspoon baking powder
2 teaspoons orange peel, finely diced
1/2 cup dried cranberries

First preheat your oven to 400F, while your oven is heating up blend together the orange juice concentrate, eggs, coconut milk, almond extract, salt and honey. In a separate bowl combine the coconut flour with baking powder. Once combined whisk into the batter until there are no lumps. Now it's time for the zest! Fold in the orange peel and cranberries, mix well. Pour batter into greased muffin cups and bake for 18 to 20 minutes. This will make 6 muffins.

Walnut Raisin Muffins
1/4 cup sifter organic coconut flour
2 tablespoons melted butter
2 tablespoons milk
3 eggs
3 tablespoons honey

1/4 teaspoon salt
1/4 teaspoon vanilla
1/4 teaspoon baking powder
1/3 cup raisins
1/3 cup chopped walnuts

Delicious healthy snack reminiscent of trail mix. Preheat oven to 400F then blend together eggs, butter, coconut milk, vanilla, salt and honey. In a separate bowl combine your coconut flour with baking powder until well mixed, then whisk into the batter until all lumps are worked out. Next add in the special ingredients; walnuts and raisins. A sprinkle of cinnamon doesn't hurt. Pour into greased muffin cups and bake for 15 minutes. This will make 6 muffins.

Chapter 3

Savory Dish Recipes

Meatloaf

2 tablespoons coconut flour
1 egg
1 teaspoon salt
1/4 teaspoon ground black pepper
1/2 teaspoon basil
1/2 teaspoon oregano
8 ounce tomato sauce
1 tablespoon apple cider vinegar
1 tablespoon agave
1 clove garlic, minced
1/4 of a large onion, diced
5 baby carrots, chopped
1 celery stalk, chopped
1 lb ground beef

Preheat oven to 350F. You will need a large bowl. Start by beating the egg, then mix all of the ingredients together, except the ground beef together. After everything is mixed well add the ground beef and mix well. Form the loaf in the middle of a 9x13 pan and bake for 35 minutes.

Fried Fish

1/3 cup coconut flour
4 fish filets
1 cup buttermilk
1/4 cup corn meal
Salt and pepper to taste
Cayenne pepper to taste
4 tablespoons of coconut oil
Fresh lemon juice

In a mixing bowl combine flours and spices together. Fill another bowl with the buttermilk. Soak each filet in the buttermilk then dredge in the flour mixture. Cover each filet, front and back, completely. Heat a medium skillet over medium heat. Pour 2 tablespoons of coconut oil and fry each fish filet on both sides until opaque and flakes easily. Top it off with fresh squeezed lemon juice and serve right away.

Fried Chicken

1/2 cup coconut flour
2 eggs
1 whole cut chicken
1/2 cup tapioca flour or cornstarch
1 teaspoon garlic salt
1/2 teaspoon ground black pepper
Coconut oil for frying

Preheat oven to 375F. You will need to bowls. In the first one combine coconut flour, tapioca flour, garlic salt, and ground black pepper. In the second bowl, beat the eggs and set aside. Take each piece of chicken and dip it in the egg, then cover the chicken in the flour mixture. Heat a large frying pan to medium heat and fill with coconut oil. Put each piece of chicken in the oil for about 3 minutes per side. Next you will need to bake the chicken until it is fully cooked. Transfer the chicken pieces to a cookie sheet and bake for 35-45 minutes.

Beef Stroganoff

3 tablespoons of coconut flour
3 tablespoons of coconut oil
5 cloves of garlic, minced
1 large onion, chopped
3.5 pounds or sirloin tip roast
Salt and pepper
3-8 ounce containers of sliced mushrooms
1 tablespoon dill weed
1/2 cup red wine
1/2 cup beef or chicken stock
2 tablespoons coconut water vinegar
1 tablespoon Worcestershire sauce
1 tablespoon tapioca flour
1-16 ounce container of sour cream
1/2 cup chopped fresh parsley

Use coconut oil to grease the bottom of the slow cooker pot. Heat 3 tablespoons of coconut oil in a medium skillet and sauté garlic and onion until brown. In a small bowl combine red wine, stock, coconut water, vinegar, Worcestershire sauce, tapioca and coconut flour and set aside. Place the beef strips into the slow cooker and season with salt and pepper. Spread the onion and garlic on top of the beef. Next you will add the mushrooms and dill weed. Pour the red wine mixture over the beef and cover. Cook on high for 2 hours and then on low for 1 1/2 hours. During the last hour stir in sour cream and parsley. Cook the beef until it is tender and cooked all the way through.

Coconut Crusted Halibut

2 cups of coconut flour
4 eggs
3 cups shredded coconut
2 tablespoons old bay seasoning
1 tablespoon white pepper
1 table spoon black pepper
1 tablespoon cumin
1 tablespoon thyme
6 tablespoons coconut oil
6 halibut fillets

Preheat skillet over medium heat. You will need a shallow dish, spread the coconut flour in it. Next whisk your eggs in a wide bowl. Third, combine and mix well shredded coconut flakes, old bay seasoning, white pepper, fresh ground black pepper, cumin, and thyme. Add coconut oil to skillet while rinsing and patting down your fish fillets. Roll the fish in coconut flour, dip in egg and then coat with the coconut mixture. Place each fillet in the hot oil until they turn a golden brown on both sides. Keep these warm in the oven as you fry.

Herb and Tomato Pizza

1/2 cup sifted coconut flour
3 eggs
1 clove garlic
1 cup whole milk
1/2 teaspoon baking powder
1/2 teaspoon salt
1 teaspoon dried oregano
1 teaspoon dried basil
Tomato sliced, pizza sauce (optional)
1 ounce mozzarella cheese (optional)

Preheat oven to 375 degrees. Use a medium sized bowl to mix in milk and garlic. Combine remaining ingredients into the milk mixture. The dough will be a thin consistency that should be spread able but not extremely runny. Spread evenly on a pizza pan or cookie sheet lined with parchment paper and bake for 12 to 20 minutes. When edges turn brown it is ready. Flip crust over to remove parchment paper and you are ready to top your pizza with your favorite toppings. We recommend tomato sauce, mozzarella cheese, oregano and slices of tomato.

Spinach Soufflé

1 tablespoon coconut flour
1 cup cottage cheese
3 eggs, lightly beaten
3 tablespoons coconut oil or butter, melted
1 cup shredded cheddar cheese
10 ounce spinach, defrosted and drained

This is a nutritious and satisfying dish. Start by preheating your oven to 350 degrees F and greasing a loaf pan. In a bowl you will mix the cottage cheese, coconut oil, coconut flour and eggs. After those are mixed well add the cheese and spinach. Pour into the loaf pan and bake for 1 hour when the top should be golden brown.

Creamy Chicken Soup

1/2 cup coconut flour
3 pound whole chicken, cooked and shredded
1 tablespoon coconut oil
1 onion, chopped
4 cloves garlic
1/2 cup butter
2 cups chicken stock
16 ounce stewed tomatoes with juice
2 chopped zucchini's
2 yellow squashes
2 carrots chopped
2 celery chopped
12 ounce coconut milk
Cilantro
Avocado

The seasoned chicken should be cooked, cooled and have all the meat removed from the bones. In a large pot, melt the coconut oil and sauté the onion and garlic for a few minutes until they soften. Next add the butter and slowly stir in the flour to create a paste. You can add more flour and butter to make a thicker soup. Whisk in the chicken stock. Additional chicken stock can be used if it becomes too thick. Mix in all vegetables and the shredded chicken. Add seasonings to taste and let simmer at least 30 minutes. Right before serving add coconut milk and simmer for 5-10 more minutes. This makes the soup creamier. Top with cilantro and avocado.

Homemade Hamburger

2 tablespoons coconut flour
2 eggs
Fresh hamburger meat
Your choice of spices

Start by lining a cookie sheet with parchment paper. Use a large mixing bowl to combine eggs, meat, salt, pepper, your additional spices and the coconut flour. Use your hands to mix it together really well. Make balls of the meat mixture in your hands and place between two pieces of parchment paper to create desired thickness. Use your fingers to flatten the hamburger. They are ready to be frozen for future use or barbecued now!

Coconut Battered Shrimp

2 1/2 tablespoons of coconut flour
2 eggs
1/4 teaspoon of baking powder
Dash of salt and pepper
1 teaspoon of your preferred seasoning
8 medium sized peeled shrimp
1/2 cup of unsweetened coconut flakes

Preheat your deep fryer to 325F. Whisk together eggs in a bowl and then add coconut flour, baking powder, salt, pepper and additional seasoning. Mix the batter very well until it is smooth. Use another bowl to fill with coconut flakes. Take each shrimp and dip it in the batter, followed by the coconut flakes. Repeat until all the shrimps have been dredged. Then it is time to fry them! Place 4 shrimp in the fryer and flip when the underside is golden brown. The shrimp is done when it floats to the top and both sides are golden brown.

Chapter 4

A Healthier Way to Celebrate: Cakes and Cupcakes

White Cake

2 cups coconut flour
12 eggs (yes you read it right, 1 dozen eggs)
2 cups coconut milk
3/4 cup honey
2 teaspoon vanilla extract
1/2 teaspoon coconut extract
1/2 teaspoon orange extract
1/2 teaspoon baking soda
1/4 teaspoon unrefined sea salt
Coconut oil

Preheat your oven to 350F. Grease and spread coconut flour on 2- 8 inch cake tins. Beat all 12 eggs, two cups of coconut milk, 3/4 cup of honey, vanilla, coconut extract and orange extract until smooth and creamy. Next mix in 2 cups of coconut flour, a 1/2 teaspoon baking soda and 1/4 teaspoon of sea salt into the egg mixture. Beat until you have a smooth batter. Pour the batter into the two cake tins and smooth the batter with a spatula. Bake for about 40 minutes, keeping an eye out for when the cake separates from the sides of the tin. Allow the cake to cool completely before removing the frosting.

Chocolate Cake

2 cups coconut flour
1 cup unsweetened cocoa powder
10 eggs
1 cup butter softened
1 2/3 cup sugar
1/2 teaspoon vanilla extract
1 1/2 teaspoon baking soda
1/2 teaspoon baking powder
1 teaspoon salt
1 1/2 cup milk
Coconut oil

Preheat your oven to 350 degrees F and grease 2-8 inch layer pans with oil and then sprinkle them with cocoa powder. Next beat together the softened butter and sugar for about 2 minutes. Next add the eggs, one at a time and beat on high speed with the electric mixer. Next mix in the vanilla. In a separate bowl combine the dry ingredients together. Add the milk and dry ingredients into the wet ingredients alternating between each. Mix on high for about 5 minutes and then pour into pans and bake for 30-35 minutes.

Carrot Cake

1 cup coconut flour
1/2 cup raisins
1/2 cup coconut milk
12 eggs
1 cup pumpkin puree or applesauce
1 teaspoon vanilla
2 tablespoons of cinnamon
1/2 teaspoon nutmeg, cloves and sea salt
1 teaspoon baking soda
1 teaspoon baking powder
1 cup crushed pineapple
3/4 cup coconut oil
2 cups grated carrots
1/2 cup shredded coconut
1/4 cup honey
Extra coconut milk to thin if needed

Icing:
1 package of cream cheese
1/4 cup butter
1/4 cup honey
1 teaspoon vanilla

Preheat your oven to 350F and grease a 9x13 baking dish with butter or coconut oil. You'll start by combining raisins, coconut milk and warm water and blending until smooth to create a sweet liquid base for the batter. Next you will beat in the 12 eggs and vanilla blending until smooth. Pour this mixture into a large bowl and add coconut flour, cinnamon, nutmeg, cloves, sea salt, baking powder and baking soda mixing all ingredients together until smooth. Mix in coconut oil. Next by hand stiff in grated carrot, shredded coconut, crushed pineapple and honey. You should be able to spread and pour the batter, if it is too thick, add in coconut milk to thin it out. Spread the batter into the baking dish and bake for 60-90 minutes. Look for the middle of the cake to be set and not soft. When it is finished remove and let cool. Mix all icing ingredients and spread atop the cake right before serving.

Strawberry Lime Cake

1/2 cup coconut flour
4 eggs
2 limes, bested and juiced
1/2 cup milk
1/4 cup coconut oil or butter
1/3 cup honey
1 teaspoon vanilla
1 teaspoon baking soda
1/4 teaspoon sea salt

Whipped icing:
14 ounce can coconut milk
2 teaspoons raw honey
1 lime, zested
1 teaspoon pure vanilla extract
Pinch of sea salt

Toppings:
1 1/2 cup diced strawberries

Whipped topping directions:
Keep your can of coconut milk refrigerated overnight in order to get the best results. Use the cream that has risen to the top from our can on coconut milk. Place just the cream in a bowl and whip until it peaks form. Once it has peaked, whip in your lime zest, honey, vanilla and pinch of sea salt and it's ready to go.

Preheat oven to 350 degrees F and grease an 8x8 baking dish. In a bowl, combine the eggs, lime juice, lime zest, honey, coconut oil, vanilla and milk and mix them well. Next mix in the coconut flour, baking soda and salt. Make sure the batter is smooth and all the lumps are worked out. Bake for 20-25 minutes and be sure it is not over browned. Let the cake cool entirely and then top with whipped cream topping. Let sit in the fridge for at least one hour. Top with strawberries and serve.

Lemony Coconut Cake

1/2 cup coconut flour
4 eggs
1/3 cup coconut oil
1 cup almond meal
1 - 1 1/2 cups of milk
Juice from 1 lemon
1/2 teaspoon baking soda
1 tablespoon vanilla extract
Stevia to taste
Shredded coconut

Preheat the oven to 350 F and grease a cake, pie pan or muffin tin. Heat the coconut oil on the stove top over low until melted and whisk the eggs into the oil. The next ingredients to go in are 1 cup of milk and coconut flour. Make sure to mix through all the lumps. Add the almond meal, mix, lemon juice, baking soda, vanilla extract, and stevia. If the mixture is too thick you can add more milk. Sprinkle a layer of shredded coconut on the bottom and pour the batter into the greased pan. Sprinkle some more coconut on top and bake for 30-35 minutes or until lightly browned around the edges.

Vanilla Cupcakes

1/2 cup of coconut flour
1/4 teaspoon of salt
1/4 teaspoon of baking soda
4 eggs
1/3 cup of oil or butter
1/2 cup of honey
1 tablespoon of vanilla extract

Preheat oven to 350 degrees F and drop cupcake liners into your muffin pan. Combine and mix well all the dry ingredients. In a separate bowl combine the wet ingredients and mix well. Add the wet ingredients to the dry ingredients and mix until there are no clumps and your batter is smooth. Now fill up the cupcake liners about 3/4 of the way with your batter and bake for about 20 minutes. Add your favorite icing to give them some character.

Fudge Cupcakes

1 tablespoon coconut flour
6 ounce salted butter
11 ounce 80% dark chocolate
5 eggs
2 tablespoons water
3/4 cups granulated sugar
2 teaspoons vanilla
1 tablespoon unsweetened cocoa powder
Coconut chips

Preheat oven to 300 F and line a muffin pan with cupcake liners. Melt the chocolate and butter over a double boiler over very low heat. Whisk the eggs, water, sugar and vanilla on medium high for about 3 minutes. Switch the mixer to low and slowly add the chocolate mixture. Once the chocolate mixture is fairly mixed in you can Increase the speed for about 30-40 seconds. Add coconut flour and cocoa and beat for another 30 seconds. Next fill your cupcake liners with the batter and bake 15-20 minutes.

Chapter 5

Treat Yourself to Healthier Desserts

Pie Crust

1/4 cup coconut flour
2 crispy pecans
2 teaspoon vanilla
2 tablespoon honey
1/4 teaspoon stevia
2 tablespoon butter
1/2 teaspoon sea salt

Experiment with your favorite pie filling inside this healthy crust option. Preheat the oven to 300 degrees F and use coconut oil to grease a 9 inch tart dish. Place a circle of parchment paper on the bottom. Start by processing the pecans until they are tiny pieces. Then mix in the vanilla, honey and salt. Slowly add in the coconut flour in small increments, you might not need the full amount. While the food processor is running add in small pieces of butter to mix with the batter. Take the batter and press it into the sides of the pan as evenly as possible. Bake until golden brown, about 15-20 minutes. Then remove the crust, let it cool and fill it with your favorite pie.

Peanut Butter Cups

1/3 cup coconut flour
3/4 cup creamy peanut butter
1/4 cup honey
1 cup oat flour
24 ounce chocolate chips
2 tablespoons coconut oil

Start by lining a muffin pan with cupcake liners. Next mix together the peanut butter, honey, oat flour, and coconut flour to form a dough like consistency. Roll them into balls and then flatten them out. Next melt your chocolate with coconut oil. Pour chocolate into each cupcake liner, then place the peanut butter mixture in and add a top layer of chocolate. Continue until your mixtures are gone. Store them in the freezer until you are ready to enjoy!

Strawberry Shortcake Bites

1/2 cup and 2 tablespoons coconut flour
1 pound of strawberries (de-stemmed, cored and sliced thin)
1/3 cup and 1 tablespoon of coconut oil
1/3 cup of honey
2 large eggs
1/2 teaspoon vanilla

Preheat the oven to 325F and grease a cookie sheet. You will start by melting the coconut oil in a thick bottomed pan and adding the sliced strawberries. Bring the mixture to a boil and then lower the heat down to simmering for about 50 minutes, stirring regularly. This will make a strawberry jam that you want reduced to about 1/2 cup. Let this mixture cool completely before mixing it in with the dough. In a mixing bowl combine coconut flour, coconut oil, eggs, honey, and vanilla, whipping with a hand mixer for 2 minutes. Let the dough rest for 5 minutes to allow the coconut flour to absorb the liquids. It will become very soft. Once the strawberry jam is cooled lightly stir it into the dough. The goal is to get a swirled effect. Drop tablespoons of the mixture onto the cookie sheet making round shapes. Bake for 10 minutes, until they feel firm to the touch and then let cool.

Chocolate Chip Cookies

1/2 cup coconut flour
2 eggs
2 tablespoon of honey
1/3 cup of coconut oil
1/3 cup of chocolate chips
Sprinkle of sea salt
1 teaspoon vanilla extract

Preheat your oven to 375 degrees F and line cookie sheets with parchment paper. In a mixing bowl combine coconut oil, honey, eggs, vanilla extract, and sea salt. Once mixed well add in the coconut flour and chocolate chips and mix very thoroughly with the liquid ingredients. Make 1 inch balls and flatten them down on the cookie sheets. Bake for about 15 to 20 minutes and enjoy!

Walnut Apple Banana Cookies
2 bananas
1 apple
1/3 cup almond butter
1/3 cups full fat canned coconut milk
1/3 cup coconut flour
1/3 cup walnuts
1/2 teaspoon baking soda
1 tablespoon cinnamon

Preheat oven to 250 degrees F. Cover two baking sheets with parchment paper. Then in a mixing bowl, combine your dry ingredients (coconut flour, baking soda, cinnamon). Place walnuts and apple in a food processor and process until they are finely processed. In a separate bowl mash bananas with a fork and add the apple- walnut combination, coconut milk, and almond butter to the bananas. Mix all well and then combine the wet and dry ingredients together well. Spoon the cookie mixture on the parchment paper and bake for 25 minutes.

Sugar Cookies

1/4 cup coconut flour
1/2 cup almond flour
1/4 cup shredded coconut
1 egg
2 tablespoons honey
3 teaspoons vanilla
3 tablespoons butter
1/4 teaspoon liquid stevia

Preheat oven to 325 degrees F and line a cookie sheet with parchment paper. Mix together egg, honey, butter, stevia, and vanilla extract. Next mix in the almond flour, shredded coconut, and part of the coconut flour. You may not need all of the coconut flour and should gradually add it in to test the thickness of the batter. If you are unable to make the batter into ball shapes, add more coconut flour. Form balls and place them onto your cookie sheet. Bake for 12-16 minutes, when the cookies turn lightly brown. Then cool.

Brownies

3/4 cup sifted coconut flour
2 squares (1 ounce each) unsweetened chocolate
3/4 cup butter
1 cup sugar
1/2 teaspoon vanilla
6 beaten eggs
1/2 teaspoon baking powder
1/2 teaspoon salt
1 cup walnuts or pecans, chopped

Preheat your oven to 350 degrees F and grease an 8x8x2-inch baking dish Next, in a saucepan heat chocolate and butter over low heat, stirring occasionally, until melted. Remove from heat. Mix in sugar, eggs, and vanilla. Stir in remaining ingredients. Spread into baking dish and bake for 30 minutes. Cool slightly; cut into 2-inch squares.

Lemon Coconut Macaroons

1/4 cup coconut flour
3 large eggs
5 cups shredded coconut
1/2 cup stevia
1/2 cup coconut milk
1 teaspoon lemon zest
2 tablespoon lemon juice

Preheat oven to 325 degrees F and prepare a cookie sheet lined with mini cupcake papers. Process 3.5 cups of shredded coconut into small pieces. Remove the chopped coconut and place it in a pot with the warm water. Heat a sauce pan on low-medium heat and mix the water and shredded coconut for about 5 minutes, it will become a paste. Next take the lemons and juice them. Then transfer the warm coconut into the food processor to mix with the lemon zest, lemon juice, eggs, honey, coconut cream and coconut flour. The last addition will be the remaining 1.5 cups of shredded coconut. The batter will be thick. Measure it out by the tablespoon and scoop it into the mini cupcake papers. Bake for about 30 minutes when they just begin to brown. Let them cool and refrigerate them.

Pecan Treats
1/2 cup butter
1 cup brown sugar
4 eggs
1/2 teaspoon vanilla
1/8 teaspoon salt
1 1/2 cups grated or flaked coconut
3/4 cup pecans, chopped
1 cup sifted coconut flour

Preheat oven to 375 degrees F and grease a cookie sheet. Next you will mix together sugar, butter, eggs, salt, vanilla, coconut and pecans. Mix in coconut flour and make sure to mix until all the lumps are worked out. Drop batter in teaspoon size balls 1-inch apart on your cookie sheet. Bake for 14 to 15 minutes or until lightly browned. Cool slightly and remove from cookie sheet.

Cream Tart in a Chocolate Crust

1/4 cup coconut flour
1 medium egg
2 cups almond flour
1/4 cup cocoa powder
3 tablespoons raw honey
2 tablespoons coconut oil
1 teaspoon vanilla
1/2 teaspoon sea salt
1/2 teaspoon baking soda

Preheat oven to 300 degrees F and grease a 9 inch tart pan. Combine all wet ingredients (egg, honey, oil, vanilla) in a food processor. Once thoroughly mixed add the dry ingredients and process until the mixture forms a nice ball. You can add extra coconut flour if the dough is sticky. Place the dough into the tart pan, pressing it into the bottom and sides as best as possible. Bake for 15 minutes for a delicious chocolate crust.

Fill it with coconut filling:
1 tablespoon vanilla
2 tablespoons raw honey
1 box coconut cream

Mix ingredients well and place in the freezer for 1 hour. It will thicken and you can spread on the cooled crust. Top with fruits of your choice! Blueberries, raspberries, and kiwis make for a refreshing treat.

Made in the USA
Columbia, SC
26 September 2018